2ND EDITION

COUNTRY CHRISTMAS

ISBN 13: 978-0-7935-2858-5
ISBN 10: 0-7935-2858-5

HAL•LEONARD®
CORPORATION
7777 W. BLUEMOUND RD. P.O. BOX 13819 MILWAUKEE, WI 53213

Visit Hal Leonard Online at
www.halleonard.com

CONTENTS

BLAME IT ON THE MISTLETOE

Words and Music by
TOBY KEITH

BLUE CHRISTMAS

Words and Music by BILLY HAYES
and JAY JOHNSON

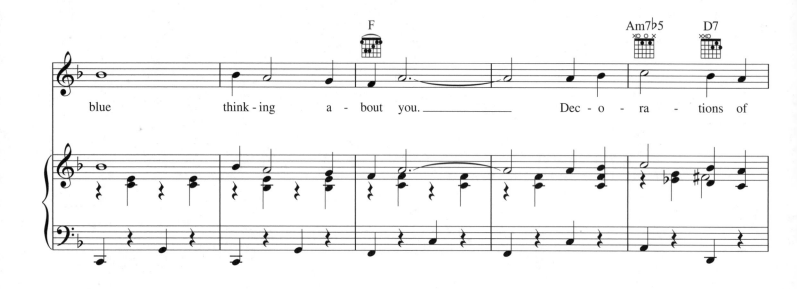

CHRISTMAS IN DIXIE

Words and Music by JEFFREY COOK,
TEDDY GENTRY, MARK HERNDON
and RANDY OWEN

By now in New York Cit - y, _____ there's snow _ on the ground. _
ca - go, _____ the kids are out of school. _

THE GREATEST GIFT OF ALL

Words and Music by
JOHN JARVIS

IT WASN'T HIS CHILD

Words and Music by
DONALD EWING II

Quietly, with motion

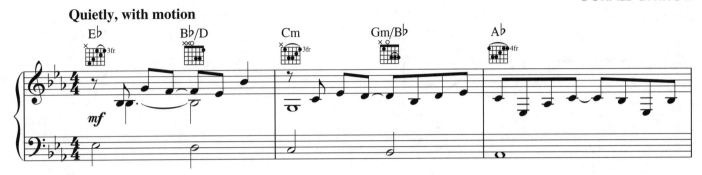

He was ___ her man, ___ she was his

and kind ___ and good. ___ And I be-

lieve he did ___ his best.

It was-n't eas - y for ___ him, but he did all ___ he could. ___

To Coda ⊕

___ His son was dif - f'rent _____ from the rest.

It was-n't his child,

it was-n't his child.

D.S. al Coda

CODA

He grew up with his hands ___ in wood. ___

HARD CANDY CHRISTMAS

from THE BEST LITTLE WHOREHOUSE IN TEXAS

Words and Music by
CAROL HALL

Hey, / Hey,

may-be I'll / may-be I'll

dye my hair, __ / learn to sew, __

may-be I'll move some-where. __ May-be I'll / may-be I'll just lie low. __ May-be I'll

HERE COMES SANTA CLAUS
(Right Down Santa Claus Lane)

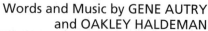

Words and Music by GENE AUTRY
and OAKLEY HALDEMAN

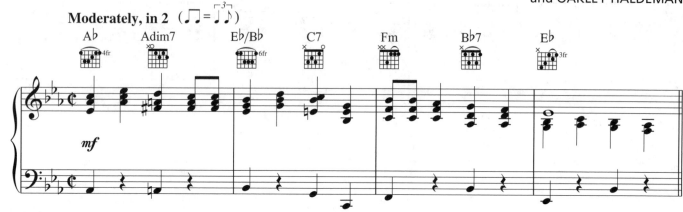

Here comes San-ta Claus! Here comes San-ta Claus! Right down San-ta Claus Lane!

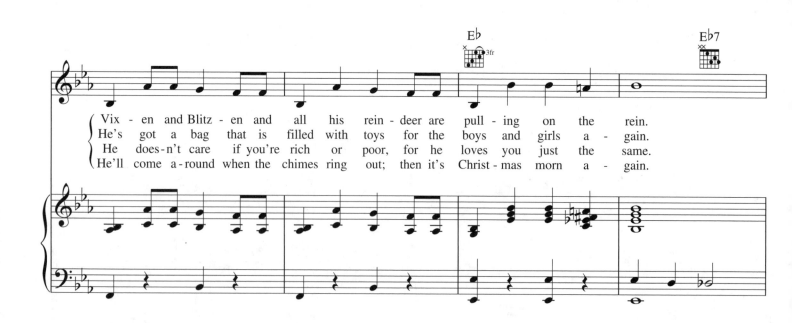

Vix-en and Blitz-en and all his rein-deer are pull-ing on the rein.
He's got a bag that is filled with toys for the boys and girls a-gain.
He does-n't care if you're rich or poor, for he loves you just the same.
He'll come a-round when the chimes ring out; then it's Christ-mas morn a-gain.

Bells are ring - ing, chil - dren sing - ing, all is mer - ry and
Hear those sleigh - bells jin - gle jan - gle, what a beau - ti - ful
San - ta knows that we're God's chil - dren; that makes ev - 'ry - thing
Peace on earth will come to all if we just fol - low the

bright.   Hang your stock - ings and say your pray'rs,
sight.   Jump in bed, cov - er up your head,   'cause
right.   Fill your hearts with a Christ - mas cheer,
light.   Let's give thanks to the Lord a - bove,

San - ta Claus comes to - night.   San - ta Claus comes to - night.

I ONLY WANT YOU FOR CHRISTMAS

Words and Music by TIM NICHOLS
and ZACK TURNER

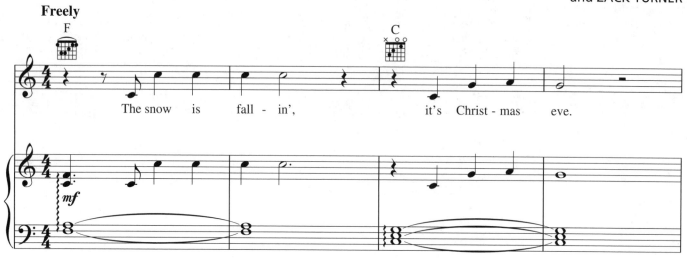

The snow is fall-in', it's Christ-mas eve.

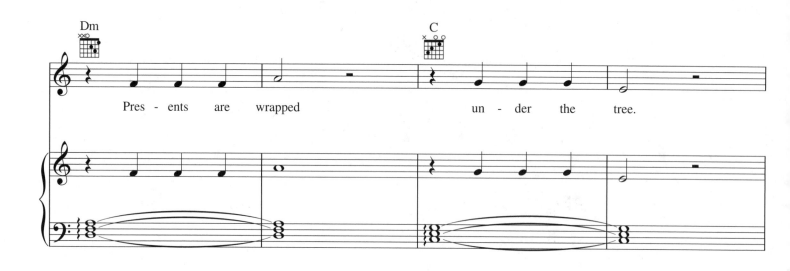

Pres-ents are wrapped un-der the tree.

Is there one for ____ me? I on-ly want

-ter to send north to the pole. ___ 'Cause

what I'm want-in' this ___ year Saint Nick don't need to know. __

I on-ly want

Ho, ho, ho, _____ I on-ly want you _____ for Christ-mas, ba-by, I don't need noth-in' else. _____ I on-ly want you _____ for Christ-mas, ba-by, tie a rib-bon a-round _____ your-self. I on-ly want

Oh, tie a rib-bon a-round __ your-self. __

I WISH EVERYDAY COULD BE LIKE CHRISTMAS

Words and Music by DAVID ERWIN
and JIM CARTER

I'M SPENDING CHRISTMAS WITH YOU

Words and Music by
TOM OCCHIPINTI

IF WE MAKE IT THROUGH DECEMBER

Words and Music by
MERLE HAGGARD

LEROY THE REDNECK REINDEER

Words and Music by JOE DIFFIE,
STEVE PIPPIN and STACY SLATE

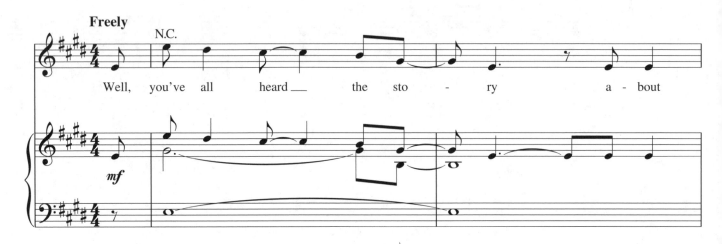

Well, you've all heard the sto-ry a-bout

Ru-dolph and his nose. But I'll tell you a

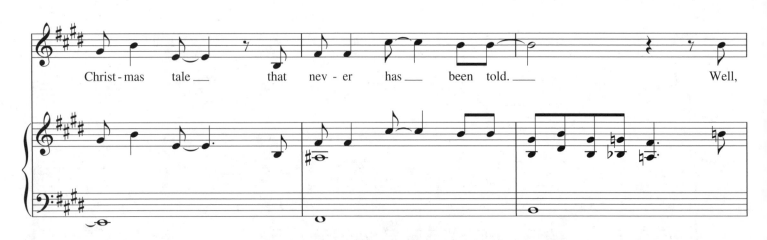

Christ-mas tale that nev-er has been told. Well,

reb - el yell___ and made his - to - ry___ that night.___

OLD TOY TRAINS

Words and Music by
ROGER MILLER

LET IT BE CHRISTMAS

Words and Music by
ALAN JACKSON

LET IT SNOW! LET IT SNOW! LET IT SNOW!

Words by SAMMY CAHN
Music by JULE STYNE

Oh, the weath-er out-side is fright-ful, but the

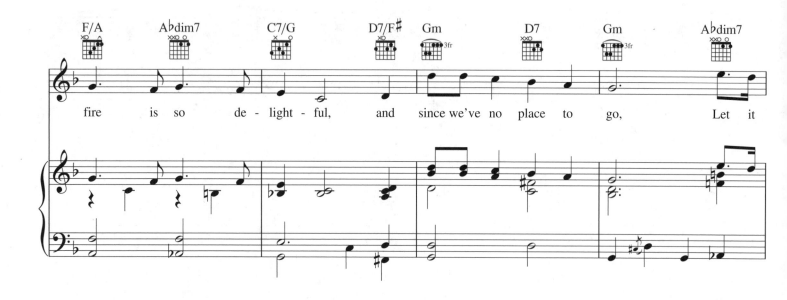

fire is so de-light-ful, and since we've no place to go, Let it

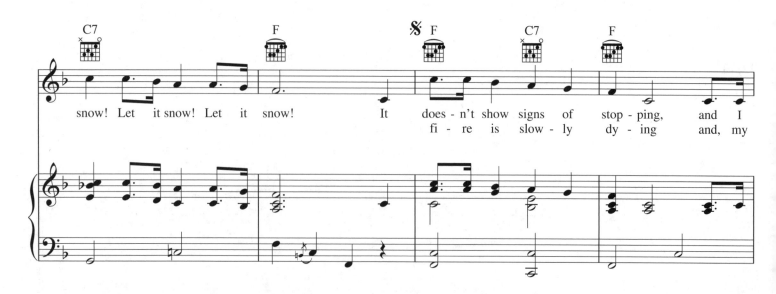

snow! Let it snow! Let it snow! It does-n't show signs of stop-ping, and I
fi-re is slow-ly dy-ing and, my

NUTTIN' FOR CHRISTMAS

Words and Music by ROY BENNETT
and SID TEPPER

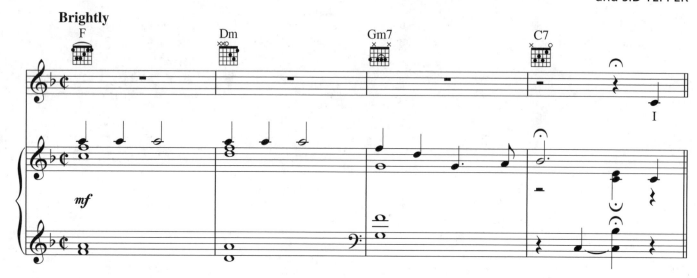

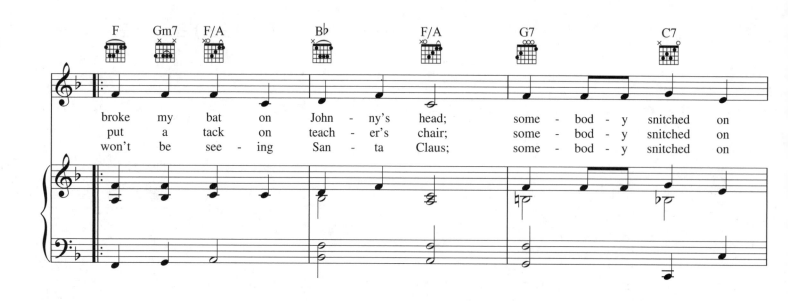

broke my bat on John - ny's head; some - bod - y snitched on
put a tack on teach - er's chair; some - bod - y snitched on
won't be see - ing San - ta Claus; some - bod - y snitched on

me. I hid a frog in sis - ter's bed;
me. I tied a knot in Su - sie's hair;
me. He won't come vis - it me be - cause

PRETTY PAPER

Words and Music by
WILLIE NELSON

ROCKIN' AROUND THE CHRISTMAS TREE

Music and Lyrics by
JOHNNY MARKS

Christ - mas tree, __ let the Christ - mas spir - it ring. __

Lat - er we'll have some pun - kin pie __ and we'll do some car - ol -

ing. You will get a sen - ti - men - tal feel - ing when you

hear voic - es sing - ing, "Let's be jol - ly, deck the halls with

RUDOLPH THE RED-NOSED REINDEER

Music and Lyrics by
JOHNNY MARKS

SANTA LOOKED A LOT LIKE DADDY

Words and Music by BUCK OWENS
and DON RICH

TENNESSEE CHRISTMAS

*Words and Music by AMY GRANT
and GARY CHAPMAN*

Christmas Collections

from Hal Leonard

All books arranged for piano, voice & guitar.

All-Time Christmas Favorites – Second Edition

This second edition features an all-star lineup of 32 Christmas classics, including: Blue Christmas • The Chipmunk Song • The Christmas Song • Frosty the Snow Man • Here Comes Santa Claus • I Saw Mommy Kissing Santa Claus • Jingle-Bell Rock • Let It Snow! Let It Snow! Let It Snow! • Merry Christmas, Darling • Nuttin' for Christmas • Rockin' Around the Christmas Tree • Rudolph the Red-Nosed Reindeer • Santa, Bring My Baby Back (To Me) • There Is No Christmas like a Home Christmas • and more.
00359051 ....$10.95

The Best Christmas Songs Ever – 4th Edition

69 all-time favorites are included in the 4th edition of this collection of Christmas tunes. Includes: Auld Lang Syne • Coventry Carol • Frosty the Snow Man • Happy Holiday • It Came Upon the Midnight Clear • O Holy Night • Rudolph the Red-Nosed Reindeer • Silver Bells • What Child Is This? • and many more.
00359130 ....$19.95

The Big Book of Christmas Songs

An outstanding collection of over 120 all-time Christmas favorites and hard-to-find classics. Features: Angels We Have Heard on High • As Each Happy Christmas • Auld Lang Syne • The Boar's Head Carol • Christ Was Born on Christmas Day • Bring a Torch Jeannette, Isabella • Carol of the Bells • Coventry Carol • Deck the Halls • The First Noel • The Friendly Beasts • God Rest Ye Merry Gentlemen • I Heard the Bells on Christmas Day • It Came Upon a Midnight Clear • Jesu, Joy of Man's Desiring • Joy to the World • Masters in This Hall • O Holy Night • The Story of the Shepherd • 'Twas the Night Before Christmas • What Child Is This? • and many more. Includes guitar chord frames.
00311520 ....$19.95

Christmas Songs – Budget Books

Save some money this Christmas with this fabulous budget-priced collection of 100 holiday favorites: All I Want for Christmas Is You • Christmas Time Is Here • Feliz Navidad • Grandma Got Run Over by a Reindeer • Happy Holiday • I'll Be Home for Christmas • Jesus Born on This Day • Last Christmas • Merry Christmas, Baby • O Holy Night • Please Come Home for Christmas • Rockin' Around the Christmas Tree • Some Children See Him • We Need a Little Christmas • What Child Is This? • and more.
00310887 ....$12.95

The Definitive Christmas Collection – 3rd Edition

Revised with even more Christmas classics, this must-have 3rd edition contains 127 top songs, such as: Blue Christmas • Christmas Time Is Here • Do You Hear What I Hear • The First Noel • A Holly Jolly Christmas • Jingle-Bell Rock • Little Saint Nick • Merry Christmas, Darling • O Holy Night • Rudolph, the Red-Nosed Reindeer • Silver and Gold • We Need a Little Christmas • You're All I Want for Christmas • and more!
00311602 ....$24.95

Essential Songs – Christmas

Over 100 essential holiday favorites: Blue Christmas • The Christmas Song • Deck the Hall • Frosty the Snow Man • A Holly Jolly Christmas • I'll Be Home for Christmas • Joy to the World • Let It Snow! Let It Snow! Let It Snow! • My Favorite Things • Rudolph the Red-Nosed Reindeer • Silver Bells • and more!
00311241 ....$24.95

Happy Holidays

50 favorite songs of the holiday season, including: Baby, It's Cold Outside • The Christmas Shoes • Emmanuel • The First Chanukah Night • The Gift • Happy Holiday • I Yust Go Nuts at Christmas • The Most Wonderful Time of the Year • Silver Bells • Who Would Imagine a King • Wonderful Christmastime • and more.
00310909 ....$16.95

Tim Burton's The Nightmare Before Christmas

This book features 11 songs from Tim Burton's creepy animated classic, with music and lyrics by Danny Elfman. Songs include: Jack's Lament • Jack's Obsession • Kidnap the Sandy Claws • Making Christmas • Oogie Boogie's Song • Poor Jack • Sally's Song • This Is Halloween • Town Meeting Song • What's This? • Finale/Reprise.
00312488 ....$12.95

Ultimate Christmas – 3rd Edition

100 seasonal favorites: Auld Lang Syne • Bring a Torch, Jeannette, Isabella • Carol of the Bells • The Chipmunk Song • Christmas Time Is Here • The First Noel • Frosty the Snow Man • Gesù Bambino • Happy Holiday • Happy Xmas (War Is Over) • Hymne • Jesu, Joy of Man's Desiring • Jingle-Bell Rock • March of the Toys • My Favorite Things • The Night Before Christmas Song • Pretty Paper • Silver and Gold • Silver Bells • Suzy Snowflake • What Child Is This • The Wonderful World of Christmas • and more.
00361399 ....$19.95

HAL LEONARD COUNTRY DECADE SERIES

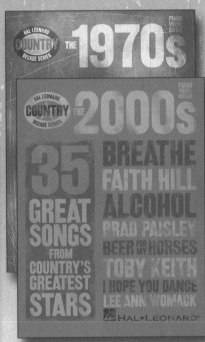

THE 1950s

50 country golden oldies, including: Ballad of a Teenage Queen • Cold, Cold Heart • El Paso • Heartaches by the Number • Heartbreak Hotel • Hey, Good Lookin' • I Walk the Line • In the Jailhouse Now • Jambalaya (On the Bayou) • Sixteen Tons • Tennessee Waltz • Walkin' After Midnight • Your Cheatin' Heart • and more.
00311283 Piano/Vocal/Guitar $14.95

THE 1960s

50 country hits, including: Act Naturally • Crazy • Daddy Sang Bass • D-I-V-O-R-C-E • Folsom Prison Blues • Harper Valley P.T.A. • I've Got a Tiger by the Tail • King of the Road • Mama Tried • Okie from Muskogee • Ring of Fire • Walk on By • Wichita Lineman • and more.
00311284 Piano/Vocal/Guitar $14.95

THE 1970s

41 songs, including: All the Gold in California • Coal Miner's Daughter • Country Bumpkin • The Devil Went to Georgia • The Gambler • Another Somebody Done Somebody Wrong Song • If We Make It Through December • Lucille • Sleeping Single in a Double Bed • and more.
00311285 Piano/Vocal/Guitar $14.95

THE 1980s

40 country standards, including: All My Ex's Live in Texas • The Chair • Could I Have This Dance • Coward of the County • Drivin' My Life Away • Elvira • Forever and Ever, Amen • God Bless the U.S.A. • He Stopped Loving Her Today • I Was Country When Country Wasn't Cool • Islands in the Stream • On the Road Again • Tennessee Flat Top Box • To All the Girls I've Loved Before • What's Forever For • You're the Reason God Made Oklahoma • and more.
00311282 Piano/Vocal/Guitar $14.95

THE 1990s

40 songs, including: Achy Breaky Heart (Don't Tell My Heart) • Amazed • Blue • Boot Scootin' Boogie • Down at the Twist and Shout • Friends in Low Places • The Greatest Man I Never Knew • He Didn't Have to Be • Here's a Quarter (Call Someone Who Cares) • Man! I Feel like a Woman! • She Is His Only Need • Wide Open Spaces • You Had Me from Hello • You're Still the One • and more.
00311280 Piano/Vocal/Guitar $16.95

THE 2000s

35 contemporary country classics, including: Alcohol • American Soldier • Beer for My Horses • Blessed • Breathe • Have You Forgotten? • I Am a Man of Constant Sorrow • I Hope You Dance • I'm Gonna Miss Her (The Fishin' Song) • It's Five O'Clock Somewhere • Long Black Train • No Shoes No Shirt (No Problems) • Redneck Woman • Where the Stars and Stripes and the Eagle Fly • Where Were You (When the World Stopped Turning) • and more.
00311281 Piano/Vocal/Guitar $16.95

Prices, contents and availability subject to change without notice.

FOR MORE INFORMATION, SEE YOUR LOCAL MUSIC DEALER, OR WRITE TO:

HAL•LEONARD® CORPORATION

7777 W. BLUEMOUND RD. P.O. BOX 13819 MILWAUKEE, WI 53213

Visit Hal Leonard online at
www.halleonard.com